"KEEP IT SIMPLE"

I seek my **JESUS** in his heavenly temple,
learn to turn it over daily & **KEEP IT SIMPLE**.
I live for **TODAY** & not tomorrow,
when I plan ahead, it just brings such sorrow!

Through these poems, you can seek some answers,
through these questions you can find solutions.

Russell D. Jenkins
WITH
Lisa Edwards

SCRIPTURES

John 3:16 For God so loved the world, that He gave his only begotten Son, that whoever believes in Him shall NOT perish, but have eternal life.

John 10:27 The sheep that are my own, hear and are listening to my voice, I know them and they follow my voice.

Hebrews 13:8 JESUS CHRIST...the same yesterday and today and forever.

-

NIV Bible

People, me included, always knew that the Bible was always talking about "them" but now I know....we are them and you are who Jesus loves, just love Him back. You have a whole lot to gain and nothing to lose but pain, misery and a lot of loneliness. If it worked for me, it can and will work for you.

Russell D. Jenkins

DEDICATION

To God first and foremost!

My parents: Phillip & Jeanette Jenkins

Daughter and family: Derek & Jessica Greene

Grandchildren: Dylan & Caroline

Sister and family: Tom & Phyllis Hildenbrand, Maegan, Krystle & Jeremy

Grandparents: James & Barbra Richardson, Ruth Pauline Jenkins

Also Christopher, Courtney, Ashley & Joseph

Love to all great nieces and nephews

All family and friends for their love and prayers

Lisa: My beautiful and God fearing friend

Drew: Thanks for letting Lisa work with me on this book

Dougypewww & Julia, I love you!

"My love and heart goes out to ALL the above mentioned."

Russell D. Jenkins

Any addict or alcoholic who feels "too far gone", you now have hope. Anyone who can relate to what I have written:

"THIS BOOK IS FOR YOU"

Love you,

Russell D. Jenkins

CONTENTS

46.
Mount Up & Ride On
47.
Learn To Listen
48.
The Flame Is Burning
49.
Recover & Discover
50.
Keep On Steppin
51.
Saved In Time
52.
Action Time
53.
Show Up & Grow Up
54.
Not Just A Game
55.
All Or Nothing
56.
From Dawn To Midnight
57.
Climb The Mountains
58.
Keep On Climbing
59.
Pain Or Freedom, Up To You
60.
Hand It To Jesus
61.
Dream

Author's Note

I grew up in a nice neighborhood, good family, taught right from wrong. I was above average in football and track also pretty good in baseball. I started off smoking pot & didn't even really like the taste of alcohol, but I liked the results. I made the All-Star team in baseball. I placed in all track meets. Had lots of friends and always had a girlfriend. As I got older, pot became more and more a part of my life. After my freshman year I gave up football. It got to where I was smoking weed 7 days a week. Still didn't drink that often. Then I got into a car wreck, was in a coma for 28 days. Had to learn how to walk and talk again. I was at age 16 and couldn't understand my life now. When I went back to school, I was not ready inside for what was going to happen. I actually started taking pills offered to me at school. Next thing you know, I'm using cocaine, crystal meth & even skipping school. My addiction got into full swing. I stole money from my parents to get high. I wrote checks and signed my Dad's name. Oh yes, I even started to like drinking to keep from looking at me. I got put in a 12-step program, did not work. Hospital, did not work. I was in and out trying to get help in 12-step programs for years. At age 44, I went to a church and God fell on me. I got baptised and felt the presence of the Holy Spirit in me. After this happened, the compulsion and obsession to drink and use was lifted off of me. I went from a drug addict, alcoholic, liar, cheater, con-man with a lonely lost soul to who I am today. Now I serve Jesus on a daily basis. I am honest, loving, giving and blessed by God above to share my life and recovery with other people on a daily occurrence. May God be with you.

Love,

Russell D. Jenkins

1
Keep It Simple

As for today, who is your king?
Is it Jesus, or is He wearing a wedding ring.
Study with God now every day,
He will put in your heart now what to say.

I learn from mistakes, I have to put God in control,
each day that happens, He gets deeper in my soul.
I can travel from here to the beach,
and my Savior is right in reach.

God will touch the ones on the corner looking for thrills,
even to the ones in the Hollywood hills.
It doesn't really matter the time or the place,
just cry out to God and seek His grace!

People have gotten touched by Jesus while riding in the
car,
even know a few who are at the bar!
All I can say is just allow Him inside,
it might get bumpy, but will be a secure ride.

Seeking the love of Jesus, you cried so loud,
your friends and family for today they are so proud.

Rusty

Keep It Simple

1. How far into the future do you plan?

2. Do you allow God to use you in any location?

3. Who is in the driver's seat today?

4. Who is proud of you today?

Notes:

_____

_____

_____

_____

_____

_____

_____

2
Peace In Paradise

Yes, I've learned to live on a prayer,
better than just living & being a "player"!!
Listening to others, I was just letting the wind blow,
they could talk & talk & never reach my soul!!

When at my weakest, Jesus showed me how,
best thing I could do was learn to love me now!!
Learning how to survive in this small town,
let go & listen, and stand on solid ground!!

Life today is good for me,
learn to accept & just let it be!!
Life has gotten better & I'm not surprised,
no longer living on them ol' lies!!

Today inside it feels like "peace in paradise",
life was once a gamble, like rolling the dice!!
Turn It ALL over & get a helping hand,
making those changes was ol' so grand!!

Today I can laugh when I feel amused,
have direction today & not confused!!
Oh! My Jesus is one-of-a-kind,
He saved my life when I was so, so, blind.

Rusty

Peace In Paradise

1. Are you playing with God or praying to God?

2. Do you love yourself?

3. How are you on acceptance today?

4. Human glasses or Godly glasses today?

    Notes:

    _____
    _____
    _____
    _____
    _____
    _____
    _____

3
Surrender

Being a kid, you had to mow some yards,
even played poker when you dealt the cards.
Even like the results, as you taste the beer,
drank the 12 pack & had no fear!

Then you went overboard & drank some whiskey,
fighting guys twice your size, wasn't too risky!
Then you got cooler as you smoke that pot,
thought you were cool in the parking lot.

Party, party, was the weekend game,
just raising HELL & felt no shame.
Cocaine & crystal meth arrived on time,
now you got into a life of crime!

Next thing you know, you're just oh! So lost,
now my body started paying the cost.
Reaching out for help & nobody there,
now all my drug , I didn't dare stare.

"Please! God save me cause I am at the end,"
then something inside He surely did send.
Went to the altar & fell out in the Spirit,
Oh! My God loves me & I did hear it!

Rusty

Surrender

1. Have you fallen (to your knees) yet?

2. Is the Holy Spirit in you?

3. Do you still have your old friends?

4. Are you a lonely person?

Notes:

_____
_____
_____
_____
_____
_____
_____

4
Starting Over

When Christ touches you, you feel brand-new,
no more running & living the blues.
Don't get lazy, got to stay on the trail,
walk with Christ daily & don't get derailed.

When you get up start with a prayer,
give it all to Him, for you He does care.
If you mess up, you just start all over,
you can't go on luck, like a 4-leaf clover.

Don't start pouting & say poor me,
prayers to Jesus, is how you pay your fee.
Don't fall into guilt & shame,
cause with Satan, that is part of his game.

We all make mistakes but we continue to drive,
cause my walk with Jesus, I know I will stay ALIVE!
People you talk to don't always catch on,
continue to pray with them, even by phone!

You can't make people go from wrong to right,
when Jesus touches them they will see the light.
We continue to work the Spirit in the sky,
people not convinced, I don't see why.
They live on pride & ego which are both a big lie!

Rusty

Starting Over

1. Do you remember when the quilt got out of control?

2. Do you have any excuses left?

3. Do you search the Bible for directions in life?

4. Have you felt the light of Jesus?

Notes:

_____
_____
_____
_____
_____

5
Give Up!

You can be wheeler & you can be a dealer,
you can also turn to Christ, and meet the mighty healer!
You can snooze, and you can booze,
BUT turn to Christ, and you will not lose!

Live on cheap thrills, while you take the pills,
or turn it over to Jesus because He's known to heal!
People think they're cool as they snort that line,
but give it ALL to Jesus & you start to shine!

Think they got it going as they smoke that weed,
things are going better, when Jesus plants a seed!
See the stars go by, got the needle in your arm,
when you got Jesus, you're not looking for no harm!

Go in the store & grab a 12 pack,
beer is not the answer, cause Jesus has your back!
Make up reasons to go smoke & drink,
live right with God and you will not sink!

I live a good life because Jesus paid the price,
without all the above, my life has gotten nice.
Used to live in addiction & never looked above,
now my friends & my family, we just live in LOVE.

Rusty

Give Up!

1. Have you felt any healing from Christ?

2. Can you walk away from temptation?

3. Do you ever go on blind faith?

4. Do you and your family live in love?

Notes:

_____

_____

_____

_____

_____

_____

6
Day By Day

At times we wake up in a bad mood,
don't get started & be real rude.
Study the Bible & your mind stays sound,
don't get lazy & play around.

Time to go to work & travel down the road,
talk to your Jesus & lighten the load.
Going through life you try & make an impact,
but the Spirit inside is jam-packed.

Pride & ego yes, it thinks it has power,
but I will take my Jesus on any given hour.
People can tell you who you are & even describe,
can't touch me now cause I'm part of Jesus' little tribe.

Some people God is good, in the way they appear,
they have a major meltdown cause they can't handle
their fear!
With material things their love was manifested,
married a year caused their loyalty was tested.

Couldn't make it with alcohol & just by sipping,
had to turn to Christ, cause my soul I was whipping!
We did things to fit in and just be cool,
but the bottom line, I was playing a fool.

Rusty

Day By Day

1. Do you pray when you wake-up?

2. Do you ever get mad in traffic?

3. Have you gotten rid of pride and ego?

4. Can people see Jesus in you by your actions?

Notes:

_____

_____

_____

_____

_____

_____

_____

7
Strength

Yes, with Christ, we can All be strong,
Christ is our Savior & He is on the throne.
You know with Jesus we can have such peace,
surrender & give in & sins they shall cease.

Holy Spirit is waiting to just come inside,
hold on tight now, and enjoy the ride.
God is there for us as we go into battle,
we stand on His strength & we will not rattle.

Christ you're my Savior, so help me do right,
you are there to protect me both day & night.
Jesus, Jesus, I pray to Thee,
I love when you sit there & talk to me.

Holy Spirit speak through me when people start to yell,
turn to them with love & don't raise no hell.
God you're my Father so help me walk your way,
you speak through me when I don't know what to say!

Your love, your mercy & mostly your Grace,
life can get tough, but with you we win the race.
With weakness I get stronger cause I learned to let go,
You touched me, You love me, Your in my soul!

Rusty

Strength

1. Who is on the throne in your heart?

2. Do you let the Holy Spirit help you make decisions?

3. How much time do you spend alone with God?

4. He defends you, do you defend Jesus?

Notes:

_____
_____
_____
_____
_____
_____

8
My Weapon Inside

Lying & stealing are certainly there for the test,
honesty & earning I learned from the best.
Spreading rumors to make yourself a star,
but really look inside & don't go too far.

Wheeling and dealing your way through life,
try & get a job & take care of your wife.
You can make quick money selling that dope,
in the end you find prison & not much hope.

Work daily, paid daily & head to the bar,
you need help from Jesus, if you want to go far.
You need to make an honest living & pay your tithes,
Jesus, knows the pain, when your heart cries.

When you finally realize you're headed nowhere,
now you turn to Jesus & you find out He does care.

You hit your knees as you feel so weak,
He comes to the ones who are pure & meek.
As He comes inside, you will rise above,
evil will be defeated because you feel God's love.
Now you have the armor to go to any length,
holy Spirit is inside & you've gained such strength.

Rusty

My Weapon Inside

1. What is over your heart? (mate, job, yourself, God)

2. Do you pay your tithes?

3. Do you share good times and bad times in prayer? Or is it one-sided?

4. Do you go to Jesus demanding or humble?

Notes:

_____

_____

_____

_____

9
Quality That Counts

Yes, He surely has cleansed my behavior,
that is my Jesus, my one & only Savior.
In my soul he won't be leaving,
He corrects my wrongs & keeps me believing.

He will help me climb over the highest mountain,
keeps me right with the Holy Spirit fountain.
He is all over me like moonlit beauty,
serving Him daily is now my duty.

He speaks through me as I do inhale,
I speak the truth is all I can tell.
Through my ups & downs with Him I keep walking,
all through the day we just keep talking!

The fire inside just keeps on a blazing,
this child here, He now is raising.
A little or a lot, doesn't matter the quantity,
just got to be real & that is quality!

Yes today, my Jesus is my boss,
He changed my soul, when I was oh! So lost.

Rusty

Quality That Counts

1. How far will you go with Jesus?

2. Do you ever stretch out a story when sharing?

3. Do you seek quantity or quality?

4. Who is your boss today?

   Notes:

   _____
   _____
   _____
   _____
   _____
   _____
   _____
   _____

10
Overcome

When temptation comes don't rattle or shake,
you will get the strength no matter what it takes!
Jesus gives you time when you must chill,
be at peace with yourself when there is time to kill.

Keep Jesus first during your working career,
in times of trouble He is always near.
Keep Jesus involved in our daily format,
when trouble comes, He will take the bat.

In time God's word becomes a part of you,
he will take control of what you aim to do.
He will work things out in your mind & heart,
begin every day with a brand-new start.

Listen to my Jesus & hear his voice,
follow Him & make the right choice.
I have peace inside like never before,
got rid of my sin & my heart is not sore.

My heart is at peace like I'm walking through the park,
guiding light is Jesus when it starts to get dark.
Jesus, Jesus, just show me the way,
to keep things right, now every day.

Rusty

Overcome

1. Do you have strength or inner strength?

2. Do you spend time just laughing with Jesus?

3. Do you have a clear mind and heart today?

4. Do you hear Jesus today?

Notes:

_____

_____

_____

_____

_____

_____

_____

11
Bless'em

Talking to my Jesus & His Bible is my sword,
living daily with Him, I get my rewards.
I really had NOTHING being a plain human being,
life is much better with godly self–esteem.

Yes, my Jesus I give him daily my will to own,
and yes in Him, how much I've grown.
On this Godly journey you do meet a variety,
but they are all good people in His society!!

From my will to His will, I do plenty of exchanging,
I enjoy life today with Him rearranging!
Down at the Gulf you can feed them by the ship,
you then feed them all & no one you do skip.

Just do God's will & you don't have to invent,
each day you spend with people, it is a Godly event!
You meet many people who feel "less than".
You pray & you know that God will "bless them".

Gather friends together and have a little sit in,
the souls of all feel they have been lit from within.
Pray for them all & give them advice,
they won't stay lost, if they turn to Christ.

Rusty

Bless'em

1. Have you grown in Christ?

2. Has God been rearranging your life?

3. Are you humble and meek?

4. Have you given Godly advice?

Notes:

_____

_____

_____

_____

_____

_____

_____

12
Answer The Calling

Share with God, even if you are not specific,
when He starts to answer, you will feel terrific.
Turning to God it becomes essential,
and with Him, you up your potential.

Reach for God cause His Love He does extend,
when it gets inside you, you won't have to pretend.
The way one lived, our lives were abused,
now we are with Christ & we shall not lose.

Serving Christ daily is such a benefit,
my heart no longer will get ripped.
The heart of God you can search & find,
let Him in your Spirit & He will guide your mind!

Life before was just falling apart,
I have been forgiven & have a brand-new start.
Misery & pain was my destination,
Now I turn to Christ without hesitation.

With Christ inside, you give your souls expression,
let go of that pride & ego which brought depression.
Everything with my past I have uncovered,
a new life now, I have discovered.

Rusty

Answer The Calling

1. Are you through pretending?

2. Who controls the will in your life?

3. Have you discovered a new life?

4. Are you answering God's calling?

Notes:

_____

_____

_____

_____

_____

_____

_____

13
Changes

At times you got to go with the way you're inspired,
no matter what you think or even desire.
You have to face life through thick & thin,
God will guide you the way to win.

At times you face friends who might be jealous,
then when you confront them, they might get rebellious!
With God in control you learn to explore,
talk to people about God & what's in store.

Talk to the needy & see their smiles get bright,
get them out of the darkness, help them see some light.
Living the right way is like climbing a hill,
can't stop halfway, for some cheap thrill.

Drugs & alcohol have taken their toll,
now allow Jesus to touch your soul.
Listen for the truth, when it is spoken,
clean the wreckage of your past, you won't stay broken.

Now your future has a brighter view,
remember, Christ on the cross, He paid are due!
Yes, He has changed my heart & my mind,
my soul is different & I'm no longer blind.

Rusty

Changes

1. Can you separate desire from being inspired?

2. In times of trouble, who do you depend on?

3. Do friends show jealousy to you today?

4. Does your future have a bright day?

Notes:

_____

_____

_____

_____

_____

_____

_____

14
Main Man

We go with Jesus, we have success,
go your own way & you will have less.
The pride inside it must be cut,
right way to go, you will feel in your gut.

Holy Spirit leading, good vibes should last,
keep going forward & don't live in the past.
Yes, you can make it & stay on top,
keep sharing God's love & don't ever stop!

Serving our God helps you feel so real,
humbling to Him, is the best deal.
Don't prove nothing by knowing how to fight,
when you do that, nobody is right.

God sent the BEST when he sent his Son,
through His blood, we sure have won!
God Almighty is our best defense,
when we are confused, He is our 6th sense.

Keep turning from sin & don't give in,
Holy Spirit will guide you, and you surely will win.
Yes, you can turn to God for a daily plan,
cause Jesus you know is our main man!!

Rusty

Main Man

1. What does it take to stay on top?

2. How do you wait on God today?

3. How do you handle confusion today?

4. When your heart is hurting, what do you do?

Notes:

_____

_____

_____

_____

_____

_____

_____

_____

15
Trust In God

Yes, inside you will live with dignity,
long as you keep turning to the mighty Trinity.
Live with Christ & you won't be frightened,
times of trouble, your soul gets lightened.

In times of trouble, your future can get bleak,
gotta get some Jesus & His will you do seek!
For your past actions, you might feel remorse,
again, turn to Jesus, He is your best source!

On the streets you felt you had your own empire,
once Jesus touched you, all the ol' ways, they did expire.
Everything God has done, you can't even measure,
now serve HIM, it is done with pleasure!

All your needs & wants, God does supply,
to seek Him out, you just give a prayer to apply.
Once you let Him in, it is so nice,
yes, our Jesus He paid our price!

I thought I could make it, so Jesus was excluded,
for happiness today, Jesus must really be included!
I know at one time my heart felt discussed,
now my heart & my mind, is God I do trust.

Rusty

Trust In God

1. Is your heart frightened or lightened today?

2. Do you feel pleasure in serving Christ?

3. Does God help supply your needs?

4. In your heart and mind, who do you trust?

Notes:

_____
_____
_____
_____
_____
_____
_____

16
Follow Him

With our Jesus, we don't control the pace,
remember at the end, we will win the race.
A friend is hurting & I'm waiting on a call,
we will talk things over & keep her from a fall.

My life is changing & can't live on lies,
some changes hurt & my heart just cries.
Friends I had before or just deceivers,
now I have friends that are godly believers!

Pray with my friends, as we sit & talk,
that helps us daily with our Godly walk.
We understand today that Jesus paid our due,
learn to live right & the Bible is a clue.

People will fall as long as they keep the pride,
you must get humble & enjoy the ride.
We learn real quick, to surrender is to win,
love and mercy, God surely will send.

Yes, in my past, my heart got hollow,
but, TODAY it is my Jesus that I love to follow!

Rusty

Follow Him

1. What do you so when you see a friend falling?

2. Do you really trust your friends today?

3. Do you really share from the heart with friends?

4. Do you make earthly sacrifices to follow Jesus?

   Notes:

   _____

   _____

   _____

   _____

   _____

   _____

   _____

   _____

17
Follow Who?

Must give a lot for your new bride,
both serve Jesus and He is by your side.
Take out trash and washed the car,
Love for your wife is way above par.
Every other weekend you mow the yard,
& Jesus tells you what you need to discard.
Then comes a time when you barbecue,
invite some friends over if only a few.

Now you have your firstborn child,
she learns to serve Christ & not get wild.
Find out now, number two is on the way,
love for both children will always stay.

Friends come over & want to drink the beer,
"no I can't do it" because God lives here!

Every morning the family does pray,
Holy Spirit in this house, will always stay!
Every week the family gets together for Bible study time,
better than my neighbors, whose kids live a life of crime!
Now comes Sunday and you worship the Lord,
I bow to my Jesus, who is my sword.

Rusty

Follow Who?

1. Do you help around the house with a good attitude?

2. Do you and your family attend church?

3. Do you have Bible study during the week with family?

4. Can your kids say that they serve Jesus?

   Notes:

   _____

   _____

   _____

   _____

   _____

   _____

   _____

18
Getting To Know

"Thank you God" for you have my back,
that you're my friend is a definite fact!
Peace & happiness for you He does claim,
let go of that guilt & all of the shame.

Yes I have to look at my daily reflection,
turn to my Jesus, and get some Godly direction.
I asked my God, "What do you see in me?"
He now helps me live with a lot of energy.

I know with Jesus, I won't be betrayed,
when I ask for His help, there is no delay.
We have to learn to give & take,
God separates the ones who just fake!

We all go through pain, during our trials,
he comes to comfort when you get out of denial.
When you give it all to Him, you feel relieved.
He answers your prayers & you have to believe.

Yes, for us God has planned the best,
and to our souls, he has come to rest.

Rusty

Getting To Know

1. Do you trust Jesus to protect you?

2. Have you gotten rid of all guilty feelings?

3. Do you mostly give or do you mostly take?

4. Do you trust God's timing?

   Notes:

   _____
   _____
   _____
   _____
   _____
   _____
   _____
   _____

19
Can't Live Tomorrow

When you first get reborn it is not so tough,
Jesus, is always there when the going gets rough.
When you are saved, it is like a guarantee,
because the Holy Spirit is living in me!

In my heart was a lot of madness,
TODAY, in my heart I just feel gladness.
Now when I help others I get excited,
when I speak, my Jesus is invited.

It is ME just speaking when I'm full of pride,
you MUST stay humble to have Jesus on your side!
I will get it all together, when it comes tomorrow,
it will never get here & your life is full of sorrow.

You broke a few hearts, trying just to be a stud,
now you feel so lonely & your hearts in the mud.
Better get right, before time does expire,
you can really get touch with Godly desire.

Rusty

Can't Live Tomorrow

1. Questions inside or seeking answers today?

2. Do you have a humble heart?

3. Where is your Godly desire?

4. Is there a new person IN you today?

Notes:

_____

_____

_____

_____

_____

_____

20
Godly Try

I can live my old ways and face elimination,
go on with my Jesus & have fascination.
Have to give a little bit of my life for you,
learning to help others is way past due!

Used to live my life, like in the Astrodome,
now I am free & just roam, roam, roam.
I used to live like I wanted to die,
now I just learned to give a Godly try!

I love my Jesus, for my heart He has touched,
once He is inside, He just means so much.
At times I get into a real tight squeeze,
then just let go & throw it in the breeze!

When I get in a bind, I ask Jesus "What have you done?"
But I have learned to let go and just have some fun.
I live my own way for oh! so long,
now Jesus has my back & I'm oh! So strong.
I use to do wrong again & again,
now I stop myself & try & keep from sin.
I used to think I could hide in the city,
I no longer live with that self-pity.

Rusty

Godly Try

1. Do you help others and give of your time today?

2. Does stress and tension touch you?

3. Do you have self-pity?

4. Do you correct your wrongs?

Notes:

_____
_____
_____
_____
_____
_____
_____
_____

21
A Welcome Guest

I couldn't find a place to hide in the city,
I was oh! so lost living in self-pity.
I didn't want to live, but too scared to die,
now I live daily with a Godly try!

Now, inside I must always stay prepared,
today, God is special with the love we share.
My life today I am on a spiritual quest,
my Jesus inside of me is a much needed guest.

The evil in the world is not intruding,
good things for me my God will be including.
Leave Him as your Pilot & your path gets bright,
with Jesus as a guest, it is a beautiful flight.

Good gifts from God you can and will receive,
follow it with ACTION, and don't be deceived.
Open your ears & your heart & start to listen,
receiving Him daily, is what has been missing!
Lead us from sin & help us do right,
you, my Jesus are my shining light.

Rusty

A Welcome Guest

1. Are you hiding anything today?

2. Do you spend time with God to get prepared?

3. Who is the main guest in your heart?

4. Are you learning to be honest with yourself?

Notes:

_____

_____

_____

_____

_____

_____

_____

22
Free In Jesus

My life before Jesus, I surely was failing,
now that He is inside me, my heart is just sailing!
I know the truth now, it can't be bent,
and when I do wrong it is time to repent.

Oh! That devil is such a good bluffer,
as we conquer temptation it makes us tougher.
I serve my Jesus & don't need an excuse,
because the way I lived before was just abuse!

The way I lived before I was isolated,
the love from God cannot be overrated.
The Bible for us is a perfect blueprint,
the love He shows us, is not just for rent.

Jesus taught me I was the one to blame,
the way I lived I played a deadly game.
No longer live by human demands,
now I just follow my sweet Jesus commands.
It was the best day ever, when Jesus fell on me,
battles I did face, for I could stay FREE!
People salute the flag but I bow to my Lord,
yes, with him, I have to stay one accord.

                                              Rusty

Free In Jesus

1. Do you ever feel that you are failing Jesus?

2. Do you conquer temptation today?

3. How grateful are you today?

4. How does it feel to be handpicked by Jesus?

Notes:

_____
_____
_____
_____
_____
_____
_____

23
Changes R Good

When real love touches you, so much is revealed,
your heart & your spirit are both Godly healed.
Your life now becomes just a Godly gift,
Jesus will protect you when you start to drift!

Now it is just God! that you daily seek,
you're a child of God & you are unique.
In my heart, a home He found,
and through the Holy Spirit, we are jointly bound.

With the Holy Spirit, inside you want to fly!
With willingness & humbleness you do qualify.
People have found Jesus while being in jail,
now if they're willing, they can get out of HELL!

In our life we must make restitution,
you can't do that in a county institution!
Woman finding Christ, I've seen a girl grow up,
praying for answers & not living on luck.

The world all thought you were tough & mean,
now you're well-mannered and your thoughts are clean.
Yes, the Holy Spirit, now lives in me,
that's why today, I have serenity.

Rusty

Changes R Good

1. Is Jesus the "real love" in your life?

2. Does God bless drifters?

3. By your actions, are you qualified to serve?

4. After you witness, do you continue to pray for that person?

Notes:

_____

_____

_____

_____

_____

_____

24

Steps To A New Life

Cause with God, a new life I am making,
temptation can come but I won't be partaking.
Good feelings in my heart, makes me ready to explode,
doing right with God, He will surely reload.

Yes, with my Jesus you can't shuck & jive,
surrender inside & you will come alive!
He never will leave you, no matter what town,
with tears in your heart, his love will be found.

You may have questions, he did not answer right away,
just keep on thanking Him as you talk & pray!
We think, think, think, until our minds burst,
now we turn to Jesus when it's time to quench our
thirst.

First thing you learn is you can't run the show,
surrender & acceptance will be your main goal.
Then you must remember, God can do it ALL,
when you cry out to Him, He will answer the call.
Get out of the way & let God have control,
sit tight with God & go on a stroll.
With God in control, my life won't cease,
with daily surrender, I have found inner peace.

Rusty

Steps To A New Life

1. Do you surrender daily?

2. How is your patience?

3. How often do you try and figure it out?

4. Do you cry to Jesus?

Notes:

_____

_____

_____

_____

_____

_____

_____

25
Just A Few

God has picked now just a few,
tried to save some but they just withdrew.
God is not picky, his love is surely a variety,
He will bring you out of that loss society.

There is something good in you, that God will use,
it will get much better, cause now you're confused.
Give it to God & you will shed godly tears,
and it is time to stand up & face those fears!

God wants you & your soul He will claim,
living right now, will be your aim.
Got to get down to Godly basis,
learn to be yourself & don't show different faces.

Putting your best foot forward was always essential,
now live through God and have real potential.
Now your mind & body will get back to sane,
try & lead people from the world of cocaine.

Living in God's love, yes He wants you to join,
doesn't care about your riches or if you even have a coin.
Like I said before, He only picks a few,,,
now it is up to you, what you're going to pursue...

Rusty

Just A Few

1. Do you get lazy at times?

2. Did you repent today?

3. Do you quit or keep going after you made a mistake?

4. Have you seen anybody get touched by Jesus lately?

Notes:

_____
_____
_____
_____
_____
_____
_____

26
Set Up Camp

Serving God we live on His Grace,
you remain small & don't need a showcase.
With Jesus you keep that inner drive,
keep Jesus first & you stay alive!

Today we don't live by hocus-pocus,
keep living on God's word & keep Him in focus.
God may take you out with the Spirit TKO,
when you awake, the Holy Spirit in your eyes will glow!

Reaching out to others, Jesus shows you how,
when you touch others, no need to foul.
Inside their soul you try to light a lamp,
now the Holy Spirit wants to set up camp.

With the light flickering, you can't hide it in a jar,
don't try & reach out while they're sitting in a bar.
We can go around sharing the good news,
they get touched inside and don't sing the blues!

All HE has done you start giving back,
you touch some lost souls who were now on track!
God will show you things during quiet time,
people can see how your heart now shines!

Rusty

Set Up Camp

1. What is Grace from God to you?

2. Do you have that inner drive today?

3. Have you helped set up camp anywhere lately?

4. Is your heart SHINING today?

Notes:

_____

_____

_____

_____

_____

_____

_____

27
New Person

A new way of life, is like a new class attending,
old habits & old ways don't start defending.
Godly way of living, you can't just recite,
Godly ways you learn with pure delight!

Bad things from your past, can't hold on to memory,
time to get right it will improve your scenery.
How you react, is not a major event,
forgiveness & love, humans didn't invent.

Troubled times come and God must remain,
allow the Holy Spirit to run through your veins!
Ask God to come inside and He will stay,
He wants you forever and not to play!

Don't make God to have to kick you in the rear,
followed His directions & keep Him near.
Fruits of the Spirit our love, joy & peace,
keep them firmly planted & it will not cease!

So much better with Jesus as my guide,
learn to live humble, get out of the pride.
Jesus has remade me & I like what I see,
now I have Jesus working inside of me.

Rusty

New Person

1. Who guides your life today?

2. Have you completely let go of your past?

3. Can you honestly and sincerely forgive people today?

4. Are you playing with Christ or relying on him?

Notes:

_____

_____

_____

_____

_____

_____

_____

28
Move On In

Learn to live right, as you turn to Christ,
cause you know my Savior surely paid the price!
When you follow Jesus, He will give you, your own little
style,
in times of trouble you will go the extra mile.

You have nothing inside when all is broken,
quit living wrong & quit that toke'n.
He has been waiting on you & He is not missing,
open your ears & your heart & start to listen!

You feel the heat inside & your soul gets on fire,
let Jesus have control of your inner desire.
God, help me point the world now back to you,
we all know our Savior who paid our due.

Yes, my Jesus you are my Shining Light,
lead us from sin & through you we do right.
We know with Christ we can't go wrong,
now to your past life you say so long.
All of the hurt before was for a lesson learned,
through the Love of Christ we won't get burned.

Rusty

Move On In

1. Do you turn to Christ at bad times only?

2. Do you go the extra mile?

3. How strong is faith?

4. Can you disagree with Jesus?

   Notes:

   _____

   _____

   _____

   _____

   _____

   _____

   _____

29
Tap On The Door

I use to live life & was oh! So vain,
humbly serve my Christ & with him I do gain.
From the abuse my body was shaken,
gave it all to Christ & had a spiritual awakening!

It's like scoring a touchdown & you are spiking!
Cause with His word their souls you are striking.
Yes, today I can say I am free,
living with my Jesus, the way it should be.
And actually today I can say "I love me".

Yes it took some time to really get started,
with the spirit inside I am lighthearted!
My heart to trouble, I am not leasing,
now as I serve Christ my faith is increasing.

Yes, today I can surely detect,
when I start to practice a character defect.
I know today God has all the power,
it will come back to haunt me if I lose him for an hour.

Getting close to God was like taking a FAITH course,
just surrender & the spirit will guide you with his force.

Rusty

Tap On The Door

1. When you strike a nerve, how do you handle it?

2. Do you detect evil around?

3. When someone argues, what do you do?

4. Do you kneel to pray?

Notes:

_____
_____
_____
_____
_____
_____
_____

30
Does Arise!

When the sun comes out you put on lotion,
but when the Spirit hits you, it is God given emotions.
When the Lord speaks to you He can get loud,
at times get alone & away from the crowd.

People get mad over the smallest thing,
time to step back & give the Lord a ring...
See a man talking, sounding like Satan,
try & calm the man & get rid of that hating.

Beauty in the roses & the butterflies,
keep on praying for folks until some Jesus does arise!
You love hearing the kids while playing at the park,
praying daily for your kids, & with the Holy Spirit, they
will get a spark!

Yes with my Jesus I don't have fear,
it can be at the park, or while they drink their beer.
I live for each day from my Jesus to learn,
got to do my part when he says it's my turn.

You see someone with a broken spirit,
pray for their healing, & yes they will hear it.
Some people live like they're playing a game,
get right with Jesus & lose that shame!

Rusty

Does Arise!

1. Do you have human or Godly emotions today?

2. Do you know when it is time to pause?

3. When evil comes around, what do you do?

4. Do you leave when God tells you to?

Notes:

_____
_____
_____
_____
_____
_____
_____

31
Hold On!

At times my Lord, I need to hold on,
to you my Savior till the thoughts are gone.
When they have Jesus, you can see their hearts glow,
and I am so honored to say they're my bro...

I've seen some people who have lived through a twister,
"hold on to them Jesus" as I pray for my sister.
I know there are times when life can get tight!
Hold on to Jesus & it will turn out right.

Sometimes you just feel the Holy Spirit in the air,
that is when LOVE He surely does share.
At times God will tell you it is time to fast,
he will also tell you when that time has passed.

Moments you feel like you're going under,
stay tight with Jesus then & don't start to wonder.
Sometimes you have to travel with Faith unknown,
keep Jesus first & troubles are gone.
At times it looks like a tragedy,
but I know my Jesus is there with me.
When the roll is called I will see your face,
then I live for ever in your sweet grace.

Rusty

Hold On!

1. Do you have brothers or sisters in Christ?

2. Do you pray with them?

3. Do you fast for the Lord?

4. Do you hold on to Christ in badtimes?

Notes:

_____

_____

_____

_____

_____

_____

_____

32
Crossing Over

Oh! The life I lived, couldn't find any escape,
felt my heart & my soul had both been raped.
My wanting to live, I couldn't find a reason,
summer or fall, it didn't matter the season.

I dreaded every day when the sun did rise,
the day JESUS touched me was a big surprise!
Holy Spirit & my soul, they surely did kiss,
bad thoughts I soon learned, I had to dismiss.

Now I had friends with integrity,
in time people saw good changes in me.
At church and the altar was my calling place,
where I first learned about God's good grace!

My heart & my soul now God did lift,
I love myself & others was God's good gift.
It took some years but it was worth the wait,
it was ALL in God's time, & He never runs late.

Talk to God but to Him you can't bluff,
open up to Him & you'll learn enough.
Talk & pray to God & learn to live,
people in your life, you learn to forgive.

Rusty

Crossing Over

1. How do you get out of your old life?

2. Do you see changes in yourself?

3. Was it worth the wait for Jesus?

4. Have you learned how to live?

Notes:

_____
_____
_____
_____
_____
_____
_____
_____

33
Can't Be A Pretender

Living my life was like a rat race,
now I must live by God's good grace.
The way we fooled ourselves, we were just a pretender,
now we love our Jesus, as we daily surrender.

He doesn't send it here on an eagle or a dove,
obedience to Him is how we learn about his Love.
I now must turn & lean on the cross,
I no longer live all lonely & lost.

I use to live just guessing & guessing,
I turn to Jesus now & live on a blessing.
The way I used to live, it wasn't too nice,
my Savior today is my sweet Jesus Christ.

I pray & talk to Jesus all night long,
with Jesus inside I can be so strong.
Thoughts of God are always on my mind,
Jesus just loves me & treats me oh! So kind.

Yes, it is my Lord that I aim to please,
found the walls around my heart have gone at ease.
He thought of me with nails in his hands,
now with Jesus in me, I feel so grand.

Rusty

Can't Be A Pretender

1. How are you with quick aggravation?

2. Are you obedient to Christ today?

3. Are you lonely or lost today?

4. Any walls in your life today?

Notes:

_____
_____
_____
_____
_____
_____
_____
_____

34
Must Do Right

There are times in our life that God must be firm,
don't argue with Christ, just repent & learn!
The more we study, the bigger the thirst,
as we humble ourselves & keep God first.

At times you feel that you have an overload,
Jesus will lead you, just do as you're told.
As He corrects you, there might be some pain,
turn back to His path & you will feel the gain.

Thoughts in your mind, don't let the devil win,
give those thoughts to Jesus before you sin.
Jesus can overcome them, they're straight from HELL,
talking about the people who can cast a spell.

Evil comes down in all shapes & sizes,
Jesus will defeat them, for they are all disguises.
"Forgiveness" is something we all must claim,
that way we don't live a life of shame.
Temptation my friend has desire that never quits,
overcoming action will come that the Holy Spirit lit!
God knows the right way & stands so strong,
yes, he will correct you when you do wrong.

Rusty

Must Do Right

1. When you are wrong, how long does it take to repent?

2. How often do you study the word?

3. What do you do when witchcraft comes around?

4. What is your sword today?

   Notes:

   _____

   _____

   _____

   _____

   _____

   _____

   _____

   _____

35
This Is So Sweet

It sure would be well worth the chance,
build with Jesus, a true romance.
You couldn't see Jesus, it was like a ghost,
if you give Him a chance, it will mean the most.

And with Jesus, you don't need good credit,
keep the spirit inside & make sure you've fed it!
One day you will say "this is so sweet",
the day He confronts you, & you're glad you did meet.

One day inside, it will feel like a little earthquake,
until this day He makes my insides shake!
I have walked so much, I have some blisters,
be there to help my brothers & sisters.

You have to let Jesus install a plan,
learn to trust the man who had nails in His hand.
It is our Savior today we try & impress,
give it All to Him & get rid of the stress.
Today with God it can be all real,
cause He is behind everything you feel.
He is the director & the world is the stage,
learn to have PEACE & don't get in a rage.

Rusty

This Is So Sweet

1. How deep is your romance with Jesus?

2. How do you feed the Holy Spirit in you?

3. Do you and Jesus have a plan?

4. Who is the director in your life?

Notes:

_____

_____

_____

_____

_____

_____

_____

_____

36
What Is Cool?

Escape my world by snoozing & boozing,
today I have Christ & I am not losing!
I will follow my Jesus on any given hour,
that pride & that ego, can forget its power!

They have emotional breakdown, cause they can't
handle the fear,
thought they were so "cool" with the way they appear.
We did sick things to fit in and be cool,
never really knowing we were playing a fool!

Yes, to my Jesus I have total respect,
the old me ruined my life in every aspect.
We brought people down, to bring our self fame,
never really knowing we were playing a game.
I have gotten right with Jesus & got rid of the shame.

Pray for people & hope they can hear it,
that is the one with the broken spirit!
We used to have pride & such vanity,
now I just operate in humble sanity.
Give it all to God was my first tip,
when I attended a 12 step fellowship.
I remember crying to Jesus when I got so low,
he took me to humble Heights away from skid Row.

Rusty

What Is Cool?

1. How do you try and escape from the world today?

2. Where are pride and ego today?

3. Do you try and help others?

4. Where are you at with SELF today?

Notes:

_____

_____

_____

_____

_____

_____

_____

37
Beautiful Flight

If you get caught, your image would get ripped,
but when you live right, you will soon be all Godly
equipped.
For doing wrong you are on a hook, line & sinker,
but walking with Christ, you have a brand-new thinker!

Learn to pray even if it has to be a little brief,
yes, inside you will feel relief...
Closeness to Christ, you feel it increasing,
all the bad inside, is soon releasing.

It got so good but you had no idea,
the way your HEART inside, it started to feel.
Good gifts from God you can receive,
it goes with your ACTION & how you believe.

God's loving mercy, it surely does stretch,
when you start to fall, He surely will catch.
Good things for you, He will keep on including,
as for the evil it won't be intruding.

Yes, in the Bible you can find the right verse,
on anything evil or to break a curse!
Oh! With Jesus it is a beautiful flight,
leave him in control, & your path gets bright.

Rusty

Beautiful Flight

1. Does prayer help you in your burdens today?

2. When you deal with a smooth operator, do you stay in tune?

3. Is your life's path bright today?

4. Is Christ there to catch you, when you are falling?

   Notes:

   _____

   _____

   _____

   _____

   _____

   _____

   _____

38
Holy Spirit

Getting the Holy Spirit was like a brand-new taste,
time to make up for ALL the years I did waste.
It is like my life was destroyed with a big bomb,
you can't just fix your life with Jesus.com!

The Bible has direction and it is in detail,
give it all you've got & you will not fail.
Holy Spirit now is here for your protection,
just give it ALL to Jesus & follow his direction!

While you're changing inside the devil will keep hacking,
Holy Spirit like a backpack, will not be slacking.
Jesus is the best & the best umpire,
He is the only one who can light your inner FIRE!

After you have been touched, you can't do wrong
deliberately,
part of living with Christ is about honesty.
We must show Jesus we are doing our best to do right,
and to serve Jesus we never have to fight.

Then we show in time now, that we do got it,
everything in our past, our Savior forgot it!
I am so happy, the ol' me is in the grave,
today, I am so grateful cause with Jesus I am brave!
Rusty

Holy Spirit

1. What is the special gift God gave you?

2. Do you choose to live in God's love today?

3. Do you have faith or fear today?

4. Where is your Godly potential at today?

   Notes:

   _____
   _____
   _____
   _____
   _____
   _____

39
I Am Alive

When I start my day, I go to the Holy Spirit,
when He speaks I mostly do here it.
Have to kneel & pray cause I can't look him in the face,
yes, He is forgiving & I live on His grace.

Mercy, mercy, is right there in my reach,
yes, I get so humble when I hear His word preached.
Thank you Lord I don't have to live with all that dope,
some people are so lost and yes, they need your hope.

I have found faith in you & no longer in a war,
I fly like an eagle & with you I do soar.
When the enemy comes around, at times I don't know
what to say,
don't clown around & turn to the Lord and start to pray!

Courage with my Jesus, I just start to fly,
strength with my Jesus, don't need an alibi!
Peace inside,,. It's like heaven fills my thoughts,
peace inside... My heart no longer is tied in knots.

Curves in life can be so steep,
thank God my trust in you, just run so deep.
In spite of my past, today I am alive.
You shared your love & I don't feel deprived.

Rusty

I Am Alive

1. Are you seeking the Lord today?

2. Are you soaring like an eagle?

3. Do you still have knots inside from past mistakes?

4. Who do you share your life with?

Notes:

_____
_____
_____
_____
_____
_____
_____
_____

40
Dealer Or Healer!

Doing your own thing never leads no place,
show others love, & live on grace...
Can't live in solitude in walls of glass,
with Jesus inside, you will move with class.

It is so true, your life can get low,
just die on the inside & your life will glow!
People got to trust in God's good fate,
hold on to Jesus & learn to wait.

People see peace when they look in your eyes,
not like others who live on lies!
Look at the world & say are you ready for a brand-new
me,
cause when you look at me, it is love you see.

Bump into a man who needs prayer, right there on the
street,
following God, don't be surprised who you meet.
You can touch a woman who has been a wife slave,
or touch a man with Christ, who just rode a wave.
Yes in the world there are dope dealers,
turn to Christ with hope & meet the healer.

Rusty

Dealer Or Healer!

1. Do you stay the same no matter who comes around?

2. Do you wait for God or do you go ahead and do it?

3. Can people see the difference in you?

4. Have you learned to let God speak through you?

Notes:

_____
_____
_____
_____
_____
_____

41
Get In The Groove

With guilt, shame & lies my addiction came alive,
that all changed, when spiritual principles I applied.
I went to jail & even got booked,
but now I have Jesus & with His love I am hooked.

The devil will try & get you to trip,
hold on then & don't lose your grip!
He may even try & get you under duress,
when you get through it, you shall be blessed.

Just remember with Christ you are sealed,
when temptation of luxury is even dealed.
Don't fall for the evil & you will score,
cause you know it is Jesus, you love & adore

to the people of this world you have nothing to prove,
keep on dancing with Jesus & get into the groove!
When you talk to people, just let the Lord speak,
and just continue His will you seek.

Yes, our Jesus is our daily cure,
don't fall for earthly riches & have a detour!
We no longer live in lost & found,
now we live with Christ on solid ground.

Rusty

Get In The Groove

1. Worldly worries or spiritual principles are alive in you today?

2. Have you got it going with Jesus and how is your grip?

3. Has temptation been biting you?

4. Is your ground solid with Jesus?

Notes:

_____
_____
_____
_____
_____
_____
_____
_____

42

I Can't, He Can, So I Let Him

I can't... make it when I take control,
He can... do it, as to his word I hold.
I can't...make the block without tripping & falling,
He can... and He will if it is to Him, I am calling.

I can't...read their mind, what the situation is,
He can...lead me away if it is none of my biz.
I can't...let go if I'm still holding on,
He can...lead me to help if I make time to loan.

I can't...heal people with my charm & wit,
He can...& He will if myself I do quit.
I can't... just laugh & forget about sharing,
He can...help me with the love I show caring.

I can't... He can, so get out of the way,
He can... He will, tell me what to say.
I can't...just give my human advice,
He can... and He has more than twice.

I can't...save people if I'm driving on myself will,
He can...help others, if I will learn to be still.
I can't...save myself, much less help others,
He can...and He will & with grace He does smother.

Rusty

I Can't, He Can, So I Let Him

1. Do you call on Jesus in times of trouble?

2. Do I find myself trying to be nosy at times?

3. Are you carrying God's love today?

4. Do I know when to be still and quiet?

Notes:

_____

_____

_____

_____

_____

_____

_____

43
Turn To Him

He will answer your call, even at midnight,
Turn to Him & he will help you feel right.
Pass-out on the streets, He is there when you wake up,
Turn to him & no longer live on luck.

He will be there for you when you get out of jail,
Turn to Him & you won't be headed to HELL.
When your spouse can't take it & kicks you out,
Turn to him & he could bail you out.

When your mate breaks up & breaks your heart,
Turn to Him & you & your soul can make a new start.
If you lose the job you are counting on,
Turn to him & He will listen & it don't take no phone.

Parents kick you out, for their tired of your lies,
Turn to Him, I'm talking about Jesus & He hears your cries.
Kids run away cause they can't take the abuse,
Turn to Him & your heart gets loose.

Try & run from yourself, but you find out you cannot hide,
Turn to Him my Jesus & enjoy the ride.

Rusty

Turn To Him

1. Do you ever fear when waking from a dream?

2. When you wake up, do you pray, get up, go back to sleep?

3. Trouble with family, what action do you take?

4. Who is first in your life?

Notes:

_____
_____
_____
_____
_____
_____

44
Keep On Keepin On

Try my best to keep positive thoughts,
keep going with my Jesus, & he will untie all the knots!
You can't touch everyone, you have to understand,
keep going with my Jesus & follow God's plan!

Sometimes you don't agree, but you learn to rearrange,
keep going with my Jesus, don't let your Spirit get drained.
You are free in life & don't have to compete,
keep going with my Jesus, & you will stay complete.

People will attack you with a little bit of anger,
keep going with my Jesus, and you won't get in danger.
Yes, and you they want to bring fear,
keep going with my Jesus, & hold him so near.

Temptation will come with a hot looking dame,
keep going with my Jesus, cause it is all just a game!
You keep going with Jesus, cause you know he is the King,
keep going with Jesus, cause His praises you will want to sing.

Rusty

Keep On Keepin On

1. Are you taking positive actions with life today?

2. Are you concentrating on doing service work today?

3. When you can't get through, what do you do?

4. Do you have fear when danger comes?

   Notes:

   _____
   _____
   _____
   _____
   _____
   _____
   _____

45
Be Still & Listen...

Be still... and He will tell you, when it is time to speak,
and listen... to Him closely as in Him you stay meek.
Be still...and know that God is the boss,
and listen... To Him closely where you want to get lost.

Be still...when you get angry & want to cuss,
and listen... To Him closely & don't cause no fuss.
Be still...when someone in traffic pops you the finger,
and listen...to some music & a good Christian singer.

Be still...if a man tries to start a fight,
and listen...carefully to God... With all your might.
Be still...when your children want to rebel,
and listen...to Jesus for the truth he will tell.

Be still...you're in a hurry but your car won't start,
and listen... to my Jesus as He comes your heart.
Be still...when your ex comes over & starts to complain,
and listen...to words of God & don't go insane.

Be still...while the devil is playing head games,
and listen...& Tell the devil he is so lame!
Be still...and no Christ is Lord & that's forever,
and listen...to the Lord & get real clever.

Rusty

Be Still And Listen...

1. Have you listened to God when it is time to speak?

2. Have you been angry lately, how did you handle it?

3. Have drivers around you made you upset? "Why?"

4. Has the devil played head games with you lately?

Notes:

_____
_____
_____
_____
_____
_____

46
Mount Up & Ride On

Mount up...when you're tired of running the show,
Ride on...with Jesus & he will show you where to go.
Mount up... when your heart gets heavy,
Ride on...with the Lord, till you get to the levy!

Mount up...like a soldier for Christ you will defend,
Ride on...with courage with no need to pretend.
Mount up...and praise my Jesus, in you he does live,
Ride on...and spread the word, the love He does give.

Mount up...like a lion who roars so loud,
Ride on...like an eagle who soars so proud.
Mount up...with weapons that will make you so strong,
Ride on...with the Holy Spirit & sing the victory song.

Mount up...and talk to one's who are just so lost,
Ride on...let them ALL know, the answers at the cross!
Mount up...and feel the presence of the Lord so near,
Ride on...and spread the word & don't have no fear.

Mount up...& Pray to Jesus when you start your day,
Ride on...& pray to Jesus & He will tell you what to say.
Mount up...& thank you Jesus for being here for me,
Ride on...& thank you Lord, for with you I can see.

Rusty

Mount Up & Ride On

1. Who is in control today?

2. Is Godly love alive in you today?

3. Do you have any fears today?

4. Has your vision gotten different with Jesus inside?

Notes:

_____
_____
_____
_____
_____
_____
_____

47
Learn To Listen

Learning how to live, takes more than talk,
listen to Jesus, when He tells you to halt.
Learning how to live & be open-minded,
sure there are times when you need to be reminded.

Learning how to give, with nothing in return,
do it with a humble heart & won't get burned.
Learning to live on with God as the driver,
you receive godly gifts & just get wiser.

Learning to give God the credit He deserves,
do what He says without getting on your nerves.
Listen to the Holy Spirit when He says "to stop",
that person there is about to blow their top.

Listen to people as they cry & give in,
lead them in a prayer, they will feel the love He sends.
Listen to God what he says to "turn-around",
talk to the straying man as he wanders downtown.
Listen to Jesus when you see a spark in their eyes,
let Jesus speak through you as their heart cries.
Listen & hold them & just be quiet,
they are letting it all out, since their heart had a riot.

Rusty

Learn To Listen

1. Are you open minded today?

2. Have you prayed for someone in need?

3. Do you ever help anyone, without telling someone?

4. Has anyone poured their heart out lately after prayer?

Notes:

_____

_____

_____

_____

_____

_____

48
The Flame Is Burning

We pray to Jesus, to conquer the task,
face it with courage & don't wear no mask!
We pray to Jesus about the situation at hand,
He will help you get through it, He is your number 1 fan.

We pray to Jesus, to help others in the way they're living,
peace & understanding and love you are giving.
We pray to Jesus, when people ask questions or advice,
tell them to "talk to the Lord" & quit rolling the dice.

We pray to Jesus, when they talk ugly & try to be bold,
love them & be firm, fly like an eagle, never be cold.
We pray to Jesus, what was being said,
just talk from the heart cause with Jesus you are lead.

We pray to Jesus, before the sun does rise,
when it is Him speaking through me, I can get so wise!
We pray to Jesus, all through the day,
Holy Spirit inside has the words to say.

We pray to Jesus, to keep the flame burning,
I'm just a child & I will always be learning.
We pray to Jesus, when we go to bed at night,
when you wake up, be strong and right.
Rusty

The Flame Is Burning

1. Do you walk with Godly courage today?

2. Do people ask you about the Lord?

3. Are you still learning about Christ?

4. Have you answered your calling?

Notes:

_____
_____
_____
_____
_____
_____
_____
_____

49
Recover & Discover

When you're in recovery you aim to succeed,
keep going forward & you will stay in the lead.
There is no time to start to play with life,
if you live crazy, it is like playing with a knife.

Yes, the old crazy days, you have to let go,
Crime or Jesus, who is guiding your soul?
No success if you ever run to the booze,
your life & your loved ones you could up & lose.

Don't try & escape by running to the dope,
turn to Jesus & find some hope.
Learn to love yourself & have inner drive,
walk daily with Jesus & stay alive!

Don't be a people pleaser for you will get lost,
don't you know JESUS HAS PAID THE COST!
You're not a Barbie doll, just for them to please,
turn & love our Jesus as you hit your knees.

Pray, to our Savior & he shall be your guide,
follow our Jesus & enjoy the ride.

Rusty

Recover & Discover

1. How often do you share with a trusted friend?

2. Do you have childish behavior or grown-up behavior?

3. Are you a people –pleaser?

4. Is Jesus your guide today?

Notes:

_____
_____
_____
_____
_____
_____

50
Keep On Steppin

the enemy can hear you like he is a disease,
stand strong in your heart & be at ease.
Life is not always like a pretty love song,
learn to own up when you do wrong.

People see your willingness & for others you show care,
get them to open up & their pain, you help them share.
People care about you, for who you are,
not your money, not your looks, or even your new car.

Show them love again & again as a Godly rep,
help them along on the Godly steps.
And for yourself you must be your own friend,
learn to ask if you need a helping hand.

Yes, the God I serve don't push or shove,
follow His steps & live on His Love.
Just keep on going & reaching for the sky,
get out of the routine of living on a lie!

When the Lord found me, I was all alone,
now He inside & has a brand-new home.

Rusty

Keep On Steppin

1. When the enemy attacks, what should you do?

2. How willing are you today?

3. Do you judge people by their looks, money or charm?

4. What happens when you push God on someone?

Notes:

_____
_____
_____
_____
_____
_____

51
Saved In Time

The sun gets hot so you sit in the shade,
decisions with God are easily made.
People in the world like to wine & dine,
but with the Holy Spirit, your life will shine.

The Holy Spirit inside knows when to rise,
don't even think about telling any lies!
When it is time, you know when to talk,
Holy Spirit will tell you when it is time to walk.

When the going gets tough, you have to be ready,
don't let it explode, and you pray & keep it steady.
You have the love of God so don't start to worry,
go on God's time & don't start to hurry!

The God I serve will forgive your sins,
He is the love of all time & He surely wins!
He looks so happy drinking coffee with cream,
but alone with his family, he is so mean.

God falls on him & says "you will be mine",
the man changed his ways & it took some time.
Now he serves Jesus & will get so brave,
his family "thanks God", for the night he was saved.

Rusty

Saved In Time

1. What is shining in your life?

2. Do you go where He leads you to go?

3. Do you allow Him to speak through you?

4. Do you have lots of worries today?

Notes:

_____

_____

_____

_____

_____

_____

_____

_____

52
Action Time

You hurt so bad, you reach out for help,
no one understands the hand you were dealt.
People say "Keep It Simple" in short detail,
no one understands how my life was derailed.

I use to hate even when the phone was ringing,
now I gladly answer with the LOVE they are bringing.
I have to learn to deal with my character defect,
really working on it has such a strange effect.

Now as time goes by it is such a sweet relief,
praying & talking to Jesus just helps me in my belief.
When I first cried out my heart was raw,
asked for some help & God answered the call.

Stay on solid ground & have Godly traction,
life will get better, ALL depends on your action!
Getting through life we all paid our due,
now let God show how much He loves you.

Follow His steps, He will guide you on the course,
with Him it's true love & there is no divorce.

Rusty

Action Time

1. Do you realize other people hurt like you did at one time?

2. Do you know today how to "KEEP IT SIMPLE"?

3. How do you deal with character defects today?

4. Do know inside that God will never leave you?

Notes:

_____

_____

_____

_____

_____

_____

53
Show Up & Grow Up

At one time I was so sure, I would die using,
now I serve God & no longer losing!
The way I use to live, it made no sense,
Jesus is my first love & I am well convinced.

Time & service I had to learn to invest,
on Godly laurels I had to learn to rest.
Yes to Jesus I am related,
my life before I was so degraded.

A new way of life I slowly ingrained,
dealt with my hearts & all the pain!
The way I used to live, I couldn't let the hurt show,
but the pain through the years it surely did grow.

To get past that, I turn to cocaine & pills,
living for a honey & cheap thrills.
Jesus is the way, to make your life complete,
no longer live a life of defeat.

To your God stay humble & pure,
but just turn to Jesus, for He is our daily cure.
This is one thing, I know for sure.

Rusty

Show Up & Grow Up

1. Are you winning or losing in life?

2. Do you have Godly morals or human morals?

3. How do you deal with HURT today?

4. Is Jesus completely in you?

Notes:

_____
_____
_____
_____
_____
_____
_____
_____

54
Not Just A Game

When Jesus chose you, that is like getting a single,
find brothers & sisters & start to mingle.
Might be bad, if you try & stretch it to a double,
if God is not leading, it will mean trouble.

Then the base path will start to get narrow,
if selfishness comes in, it will lead to an error.
Resting on your morals, sometimes would be nice,
contentment at times is why Jesus made the sacrifice.

Evil people might even try & stalk,
pray & walk with Jesus & the evil will have to walk.
You know it is bad moments when you cry & pout,
ask again for help & you will fly out.

To get a triple you have to run fast,
now go slow with Jesus & it shall last.
With that stride you can hit a home run,
Holy Spirit guide you & have some fun.
There is no pride when you hit into a double play,
being weak by yourself is where you need to stay!
The best one ever & I'm talking grand slam,
& that was my Jesus being the sacrificial lamb.

Rusty

Not Just A Game

1. Do you go above and beyond for Christ?

2. Do you ever benefit from selfishness?

3. Who benefits when you pout?

4. How much time alone do you spend with Jesus?

Notes:

_____

_____

_____

_____

_____

_____

_____

_____

55
All Or Nothing

You have to hurt enough & you have to decide,
things get better, when you go about changing on the
inside.
Thinking too much, makes it hard to quit,
give it ALL to God & your soul gets lit!

Emotions are tied up & your living in despair,
with Jesus we ALL have hope, that we gladly do share.
We all feel pain as we are growing,
since Jesus touched me, my heart is glowing!

Stealing & lying my heart grew cold,
living with Christ, I've learned to be bold.
I use to play with my heart, like another toy,
loving on my Jesus, I have found some joy.

To my heart then love was blind,
since my new start, my actions are kind.
All of those years that my life was wasted,
love & serenity it now has tasted.

My life was so baffling & oh! so cunning,
today with the Holy Spirit, I am off & running!

Rusty

All Or Nothing

1. Have you learned to take action and quit thinking so much?

2. Do you steal or lie today?

3. Do you treasure your heart today?

4. Do you run to Christ or run to solitude?

Notes:

_____

_____

_____

_____

_____

_____

_____

56
From Dawn To Midnight

Good times & bad times, we are always paying our due,
no matter the situation, the enemy will try & get to you..
Moments can happen & your thoughts start unreeling,
God takes you through the fire, and in the end it is
fulfilling!

Keep your Spirit and action, stay humble and do right,
no matter if it is at sunrise or even around old midnight.
Have you ever felt like God just let you down?
There is too much of you... Been hanging around.

Do your best in the Godly way you live,
quit thinking of yourself & start to give!
Don't get mad if things don't seem to go your way,
listen & take action on what God does say.

He may not move the obstacle & you must pray for help,
don't feel sorry for yourself, the hand you were dealt.
God is always in control, no matter the time,
surrendering to God is not a major crime.

Rusty

From Dawn To Midnight

1. When you see a homeless person, what do you do?

2. When times get tight, what do you do?

3. When someone makes you mad, what do you do?

4. Who do you turn to after you have been hurt?

Notes:

_____

_____

_____

_____

_____

_____

57
Climb The Mountain

Climbing the mountain there is rough terrain,
depend on Jesus & you won't go insane!
Temptation and sin is all around,
Faith will keep your feet on solid ground.

A *cougar* which is into stealing is there in sight,
keep your eyes on God & you will do right.
A mistress the *tiger* is ready to attack,
keep going forward & don't turn back!

Then there is a *monkey* who wants you to get all lost,
the directions are in the Bible & Jesus paid your cost.
Fool's gold will try & get you like a *snake* in the grass,
keep going forward and it All will pass.

Then you got a mate who thinks they are a *fox*,
Jesus has the key, to get out of that hotbox!
You keep on going, you're almost there,
you're moving on with grace & love you share!

Your following where He leads, the air is so fresh,
yes, he will comfort you & your heart He will caress.
Holy Spirit is with you as you pass the caves,
and all inside it, is Jesus you do crave.

Rusty

Climb The Mountain

1. Going through rough times, who do you turn to?

2. What do you do when temptation comes?

3. Do you read and study the Bible?

4. Who comforts your heart? Be honest!

Notes:

_____

_____

_____

_____

_____

_____

_____

58
Keep On Climbing

With Jesus, Spirituality surely will climb,
all that evil & bad stuff we leave behind.
With this path on earth we take some wicked curves,
without the Holy Spirit, we would lose our nerves!

Today, me & my friends, we are living on HOPE,
we walk daily with Christ & learn how to cope.
Our FAITH may bend but it does not break,
we keep turning to Christ & live on his fate.

With HOPE & FAITH, His PEACE we will gain,
as you learn to do right, you will feel the growing pains.
Your heart & action will be sincere,
you will hear God speaking & you won't have fear.

We use to live with doubt & shame,
now when we do wrong, we know who is to blame.
Things we would do just to have a friend,
now I have a friend in Jesus, who guides my hand.

At the time my heart aches & tears abound,
with Jesus in my corner, my heart has been found.
Now what do I do when I'm all alone,
that never happens, cause inside of me Jesus is at home.

Rusty

Keep On Climbing

1. When times go crazy, is it hard to be still?

2. Does PEACE Inside lead to ACTION that helps you deal with pain?

3. Do you blame others in your life today?

4. Who is in the corner with you?

Notes:

_____

_____

_____

_____

_____

_____

_____

59
Pain Or Freedom, Up To You

Some people learn about Jesus from the preacher,
He is my Messiah and my great teacher.
Some people can tell Jesus is inside of her,
at times He is best, when He is my counselor.

Yes, at one time my life I was destroying,
got rid of the wreckage of my past & I am now enjoying!
My life is much better, I'm sure my family would agree,
I can serve my Lord today & be so FREE.
Today I live on a spiritual level,
got to reject & rebuke that sorry ol' devil.

On my action today, my Lord should have a good file,
and for a lot of years, I was in complete denial.
With a humble spirit I feel I qualify,
today for Jesus I will testify!

A mate will torture us again & again,
until we stand with Christ, & say it shall end.
We go with faith & move out on our own,
but with Christ & friends we are never alone.

You go with faith & the future unknown,
the abuse & bad feelings are now up and gone.

Rusty

Pain Or Freedom, Up To You

1. Do you learn from preachers and friends today?

2. Do you really feel A PART OF Jesus's family today?

3. Do you testify for Jesus today?

4. Are you ever alone?

Notes:

_____

_____

_____

_____

_____

_____

_____

60
Hand It To Jesus

My life before was never enough,
now I am filled with Jesus' stuff.
I always lived to get that right connection,
when the Holy Spirit got me, I went a Heavenly direction!

Giving up on "ME" I did declare it,
life with my Jesus, I will inherit.
Yes, the 12 disciples they saw He had risen,
now I live with a spiritual vision!

In my spirit I hear God's voice,
He love me so much, He gave me a choice.
I am led now by His nail pierced hands,
my life TODAY has gotten oh! so grand.

Now with Jesus I just like to hang,
better than running with a doping gang!
Serving my Jesus, is part of my career,
my main choice before was drinking that beer.

To you my friends I need to introduce,
and a new you He can reproduce!
Give it ALL to JESUS & you will feel right,
with Jesus in your soul, it will be so BRIGHT.

Rusty

Hand It To Jesus

1. How is your connection with life today ?

2. Do you have the right glasses on, looking for friends?

3. Are you proud of the friends you have today?

4. Have you introduced anyone to Christ lately?

Notes:

_____

_____

_____

_____

_____

_____

61
Dream

That one good dream is always the best,
keep dreaming of Jesus & forget the rest!
Be alone with Him, when you have time to spare,
you speak & listen & enjoy what He shares!

Wright Jesus a letter & tell Him about your day,
will help you open up along the way.
See a man begging at the corner store,
give him a dollar, if you can't give more.

Wash your neighbor's car while they're out of town,
what you give, surely goes around!
Serving our Christ is no gimmick,
trying to help others, there is no limit!

Go to church & form a dream team,
& Jesus won't treat you one bit mean.
People who make it are far & few,
for what Jesus did, we can never pay our due!

Now when Jesus touched me, I got humbled & cried,
now from my JESUS, I don't run & hide!

Rusty

Dream

1. You have time to pray but do you take time to meditate?

2. What have you done for someone else and not tell anyone?

3. Are you involved with anything at church?

4. Have you told a family member "I love you" lately?

Notes:

_____

_____

_____

_____

_____

_____

62
Dream Lady

Everyone has a dream they want to hold,
is a dream they can't touch but they had to stay bold.
Dream is so beautiful, enough can't be said,
but as of right now, the dream is stuck in my head.
Yes it is a woman who has beautiful hair,
Oh! The sweet memories we could share.
When I look at her I see God's grace,
cause I'm telling you, that's one beautiful face.
Then her sweet laughter, just takes her to the top,
I know she's a dream but don't want to stop.
This dream of mine is just oh! so fine.
& Would be so honored to take her to dine.
Then I see her at church singing a song,
the dream is right there and it can't be wrong.
As the preacher keeps going she has tears in her eyes,
now my heart is just saying "bye-bye".
Then she and I pray for her life's success,
I know longer could pray for her and that pretty white
dress.
Then we really met in the church parking lot,
but now she will be a friend, but she still looks hot!
Christian friends forever you just have to treasure,
but the beauty she has, you just can't measure!

Rusty

Dream Lady

1. What or who is your dream today?

2. Do you share laughter together?

3. Do you pray together?

4. When you are apart, is part of you missing?

Notes:

_____

_____

_____

_____

_____

_____

_____

63
Dream World

Keep on living in your lifestyle,
or turn to Jesus & go the extra mile!
Keep on running & ruin your sneakers,
Jesus will call you & He don't need over watt speakers.

Get the Holy Spirit & get a God felt buzz,
it is better than living the way it was.
You can go to the beach & ride a wave,
but that is nothing compared to a Jesus crave!

Turn to Jesus & quit that running,
lay now on the beach & do some sunning!
When "the roll is called up yonder", you'll have Godly history,
better than the life of a criminal mystery.

In the past all your heart & mind did, was up & scream.
Turning to our Savior, & life is like a dream.
Yes, all you had before was a lot of sorrow,
now Jesus is the one with good feelings to borrow.

Life in the past was full of earthly pollution,
now life TODAY you live in solutions!

Rusty

Dream World

1. Do you listen to him daily?

2. Are you riding a wave or is it Jesus you crave?

3. Are you ready for the roll to be called up yonder?

4. Do you seek solutions in life?

Notes:

_____
_____
_____
_____
_____
_____
_____
_____

64
Know The Truth

I learned to love & don't ask, why?
God-given love, I learn to apply.
When you get a glimpse, you feel God's thirst,
as you learn to love Him, you put God first.

Have to be obedient, but don't have to agree,
keep searching for the TRUTH & you will see.
God picks the ones out, when it is time,
could be a preacher, a worker, or man of crime.

My God is so real as He came inside,
now kickback & enjoy the ride.
God wants us all to push reset,
learn to be grateful for God you met.

Listen to the Lord & He will show you the way,
He will even help you with what you need to say.
Cry out to the Lord with each day that goes by,
we defeat our trouble, with the Spirit in the sky!

With God leading us, it is oh! so sweet,
I wake up daily & bow at His feet.
Me & the Holy Spirit make a perfect blend,
I will be with my Jesus when it comes to the end.

Rusty

Know The Truth

1. Do you ever argue with Christ?

2. Do you ever "thank God" for helping you out?

3. Do you deserve to be where you are today?

4. Is it okay to argue with others today?

Notes:

_____

_____

_____

_____

_____

_____

_____

65
At The Cross

When you live right, you're ready for the duel,
we turn to Jesus & He gives us the fuel!
Yes, the devil inside it has deported,
& yes the Holy Spirit has fully supported.

People in the world will keep on ranting,
but the seeds of God I want to keep on planting!
My Jesus Christ He was the first ever,
fallen for sin, He can surely say never!

From all the bondage we had to get loose,
from the ill-treatment & all the abuse!
My life at one time was so intense,
until my loving Jesus & my soul He did rinse.

On the cross, my sins He visualized,
He was there for me, when HE was crucified!
Yes, He is better than any detective,
as for my Savior, He is so protective.

Yes, my sin at one time, had me so enveloped,
but when I got saved a new person developed.
I use to be trouble & just a hater,
I love my Jesus & the best will come later.

Rusty

At The Cross

1. Are you prepared for a dual today?

2. What do you do when people keep justifying their actions?

3. Is there any kind of bondage in your life?

4. Do you love unconditionally today?

Notes:

_____
_____
_____
_____
_____
_____
_____
_____

66
Jesus Is The Way

To live the wrong way I would make a long drive,
now I turn to Jesus to stay ALIVE.
I live my life now in God's good file,
when I use to be lost & just hostile.

I live my life like a wanna be,
now inside I have dignity!
Now helping others people now do expect,
also live my life with all due respect.

I help others now to have a Godly rinse,
a phase called HUMBLE, it soon makes sense.
A man lost in the world, to dinner I treat,
pray in time it is Jesus he does meet.

When Jesus comes inside, you will feel the bang,
no longer hang out with that ol' gang!
You learn with Jesus you can't go wrong,
each day with Him, you will get strong.

Some people say they just have a Higher Power,
can't match Jesus, on any given hour.
People must have the Father, Son & the Holy Ghost,
the three work as one & it means the most.

Rusty

Jesus Is The Way

5. Are you willing to go the extra mile today?

6. What can you do without God's help?

7. Is it hard to admit when you are wrong?

8. Do you share with others how Christ touched you?

Notes:

_____

_____

_____

_____

_____

_____

_____

_____

67
Turn The Tide

When you get tired of waking on the floor,
ask God for help & have good things in store!
Holy Spirit can be your sweet honey,
just humble yourself & don't worship money.

You can make the day with coffee & friends,
get away from those people with evil sinning hands.
Turn to Jesus & rest assured,
as for addiction HE is the ONLY cure.

My ol' friends just party and dope,
now I am hearty & have God's HOPE.
Yes, I am content & with Jesus I'm FREE!
Used to run from the law & hide in the trees!

Get the Holy Spirit & keep on charging,
love & humility will keep enlarging!
Try & help someone daily & don't debate,
God will lead your action & your tongue & won't run
late.

Must forgive yourself cause we all do err,
Jesus judges right & more than fair!
Daily surrender you must always repent,
When you don't know what to pray, He will give a hint!
                                        Rusty

Turn The Tide

1. Who is the only cure for anything going on in your life?

2. Do you seek to help others?

3. Do you pray first in the morning everyday?

4. Are you FREE in Christ today?

Notes:

_____

_____

_____

_____

_____

_____

_____

_____

68
No Time For Give & Take

Drinking & doping is no way to live,
make time alone with Jesus I give.
People turn around & run back to sin,
keep doing the right thing & learn to win.

Living in darkness, leads to a lonely life,
living for earthly riches is like playing with a knife.
Your heart gets empty, just plain empty space,
until you cry out to God & accept His grace.

Jesus is the answer, so don't bail out,
learn to have courage, don't start to cry & just go pout.
Humble daily to God above,
accept His mercy & live on His love!

Trying to walk backwards, you surely will fall,
keep going forward & he will hear your hearts call.
Search for Jesus & accept His way,
the love inside, will grow every day.

With Jesus inside, I don't feel fright,
my life today, just feels so RIGHT!

Rusty

No Time For Give & Take

1. Do you ever run back to old ways?

2. Do you ever bail out when people add pressure?

3. Are you still going forward in life?

4. How are you on acceptance?

Notes:

_____
_____
_____
_____
_____
_____
_____
_____

69
What We Deserve

Time with Jesus you have to reserve,
He will help us more than we deserve.
Learn from the Bible & keep on reading,
and your soul, He will keep on feeding.

Being obedient to God is what you need,
you will be grateful in your life as He plants the seed.
Trusting in our Lord is what we must continue,
can't even describe the blessings He will send you.

Would you rather be right...? Or just do better,
sit down, be quiet & write a Godly letter.
Yes, your life you must evaluate,
learn how to give & wait, wait, wait.

After you do that, you might need to change your
behavior,
the more we will sense the presence of our Savior.
Now you get ready to make a change,
now your life you must rearrange!

Changes in your life will never be completed,
know on the inside, that evil has been defeated.
                                                    Rusty

What We Deserve

1. Are you studying His word to get your feeding?

2. Have you wrote a letter to God lately?

3. How has your behavior changed?

4. Do you know that the way you lived has been defeated?

Notes:

_____
_____
_____
_____
_____
_____
_____

70
God's Little Crowd

You search out for another prospect,
doing God's will is all you can expect.
We are not finished yet, you do realize,
be happy & be loving, and always civilized.

It hurts sometimes, like you ran into a cactus!
Good times & bad times, it's all Godly practice!
Since Jesus touched you, life is worth living,
keep praying & all your effort to Him you are giving!

Do God's will till He closes the curtain,
you will be with Him in Heaven & that is certain.
Good blessings in my life, He does conceal,
when it is time, He certainly will reveal!

They had been hurt, by people using good charm,
they have been busted & beaten & their soul harmed!
Turn & do right & go down God's good path,
why others who reject Him, will feel His wrath.

We all learn daily on the Godly process,
there is no time to play in recess.
The ones who don't make it or standing so proud,
I'd rather just be one in God's little crowd.

Rusty

God's Little Crowd

1. Are you picky on who you witness to?

2. Do you ever stop serving Christ? Just being satisfied?

3. Have Godly blessings been coming your way?

4. Are you in a Godly crowd now?

Notes:

_____

_____

_____

_____

_____

_____

_____

_____

71
He Is Consuming

When the old me left, I was not grieving,
Godly thoughts and ideals I started believing.
God taught me daily on life & how to cope,
had Godly desire & a lot of hope.
Let go of all the alcohol and all that dope.

God today is also great,
always on time & never runs late!
No courage & no faith was with me before,
now have both deep in my heart's core!

At times in my life, my anger would be fuming,
Jesus & the Holy Spirit today are all-consuming.
Friends today give me support, love, time & tears,
at times they step forward & help me battle my fears!

God today you can say is my "chief",
yes, I gave it to Him when I need relief.
At times it gets like I'm in pure desperation,
and I read my Bible for daily inspiration.

With God the utmost you can achieve,
You must surrender & the Holy Spirit you will receive.
Rusty

He Is All Consuming

1. Do you believe that God has the best instore for you?

2. Do you have courage and faith today?

3. Where do you get your daily inspiration?

4. What are the actions you take today to achieve?

Notes:

_____

_____

_____

_____

_____

_____

_____

72
Wipe The Dirt

Peace in life comes from within,
learn from mistakes & start to win.
With love inside, your heart gets full,
just do right, when evil starts to pull.

From darkness to light, when you make that switch,
God will pull you out when you're down in the ditch.
We don't go to a paper looking for headlines,
God lit us up when our hearts were blind.

Sin tries to sneak in & stays alert,
really tries to trick us when we're down in the dirt!
When they want to argue, we step aside,
we can make it in low or even high tide!

Use to in life, we would always strike out,
we learn to live right & don't start to bout!
Remember our Christ & the life He gave,
just where he could touch me & my soul got saved.

He will touch you inside when you need correction,
talk & pray to Jesus & be led the right direction!
I no longer have to turn to that booze,
Jesus is with me whether I win or lose!

Rusty

Wipe The Dirt

1. Do you dwell on mistakes or learn from them?

2. When nerves are shot, how do you respond?

3. Do you ever think of what Jesus did for you?

4. Do you allow Jesus to correct you?

Notes:

_____
_____
_____
_____
_____
_____

73
He Has Your Back

Yes, with Jesus I have the perfect escort,
cause it is daily to Him I first report.
It is okay, if you start to slack,
go with Jesus & he will get you back.

For my Jesus, I will defend,
He has given me life, when I used to pretend!
Holy Spirit will speak if you just let it,
you will find out that you won't regret it.

With Faith inside to your strength He will add,
your life will go strong & won't be sad.
You have to get rid of all that junk,
have to get stronger from your spiritual trunk.

Yes, the message you must pass on,
and to Jesus, I sing a nice love song!
Challenge comes around & with Jesus I dive,
keep sharing the gospel & just come alive!

Devil tries to catch me with a little odd trick,
Jesus now is my power stick.
His mercy & strength will come around,
as long as I let Jesus keep wearing the crown.

Rusty

He Has Your Back

1. Do you have any regrets?

2. Has your faith brought you strength?

3. Do you have a good message to pass on?

4. Do you take on challenges or run from them?

Notes:

_____
_____
_____
_____
_____
_____
_____

74
About Face

They will fall down, yes all them walls,
you will feel it when Jesus does call.
Like the waves of the sea start their crashing,
all the old habits, you will start smashing!
I just hold on to the one thing I possess,
and in my Jesus I find such rest.
I use to stay in just solitary,
now I join Jesus, in His military.
Use to have pride and just vanity,
now I just live in humble sanity.
All my defects are now in subtraction,
now I help others & take proper action.
Use to do drugs & lived on skid row,
then I cried to Jesus when I got so low.
First God took me to a 12 step fellowship,
give it ALL to God was my best tip!
Tears started coming down just like rain,
went through the changes & felt the pain.
Yes, my disease it kept me confined,
now, my old way of living I left behind.
Yes, in time I made my amends,
made it with Jesus & the love He sends.

Rusty

About Face

1. Has your old habits passed away?

2. Do you find rest in Jesus?

3. Do you have vanity or sanity?

4. Have you made your amends?

Notes:

_____
_____
_____
_____
_____
_____
_____
_____

75
Going Places

The way I lived was just like a litter,
til Jesus touched me, it is like I felt his glitter.
A sinful life is all I did earn,
now with the Holy Spirit I surely can learn.
Living with Jesus you get more than a degree,
you live with His love & your heart can see.
Serving my God, is time well spent,
God is in my soul & Jesus paid the rent.
Yes, he even led me to some good ministry,
he has touched my soul, which we all can see.
I go to a few churches, that are all just local,
but when He speaks through me I get a wee bit vocal!
Yes, my Jesus does all kinds of healing,
from your hurts to despair & even your feelings.
My life has turned into a spiritual quest,
& with Jesus inside, He is a welcome guest.
I always do feel His total presence,
He comes inside and it all makes sense.
In times of trouble & it looks so lean,
but I know he's there or so it does seem.
Yes, inside we stay prepared,
but God is so special with the love we share.

Rusty

Going Places

1. Can you see through your heart?

2. Do you get vocal for Jesus?

3. Has your hurt, despair and feelings been healed?

4. Are you on a spiritual quest today?

Notes:

_____

_____

_____

_____

_____

_____

_____

_____

76
Oh! So Grand

Hurt, pain & lies used to run my soul,
forgiveness & love with Christ I do grow.
I live with Christ & soul can't be tarnished,
cause I know today, I have learned to be honest.

Good feelings about Christ I have distributed,
the Holy Spirit has surely contributed!
The Holy Spirit touching you can surely be shocking,
His grace & mercy in your heart are docking!

At times we feel it when our Spirit is quieting,
when it use to be HELL with all that rioting!
We listen to God & we go many places,
and as we travel, we have His graces.

We no longer lie or even assume,
cause with the Holy Spirit we are consumed.
Yes, today I have nothing to hide,
cause I know my Jesus is on my side.

Rusty

Oh! So Grand

1. Do you have hurt, pain, lies or forgiveness?

2. Do you have a hard time applying God's will?

3. Are you consumed with the Holy Spirit?

4. Are you searching the truth out?

Notes:

_____

_____

_____

_____

_____

_____

_____

77
Sweet Victory

Now is the time & no need for debate,
open your heart to Jesus & start to celebrate.
God will never take you out of range,
when it is time to make a change.

Yes, the old me it did dissolve,
helping others, it is time to get involved.
Going to church, it is time to attend,
good direction & love God will send.

For your past actions you now must reflect,
time to right the wrong & work on your defect.
Time to enjoy with Jesus your new milestones,
turning to Jesus & not live in the wrong!

Just working with others is like a new promotion,
learn to live right & don't just drift with your emotion.
Look at my life today & people can see,
that I'm just living in Godly victory!

Help others with their problem whether big or small,
do the right thing & just answer the call.
Yes, I have gone through a lot of pain,
at the end with Jesus, it has all been gain.

Rusty

Sweet Victory

1. Fighting any changes lately?

2. If your heart is free, do you celebrate
   with Jesus?

3. Have you gone to church lately?

4. Do emotions run your life?

   Notes:

   _____
   _____
   _____
   _____
   _____
   _____
   _____
   _____

78
Travel To Gloryland

Running the streets, you cannot handle,
run to the light of the Holy Spirit's candle.
On the streets, you feel you lost your heart,
but go now with Jesus & get a new start.

Yes, the devil will start a battle,
but show him with Jesus, you will not rattle.
To start ALL over you must re-enter,
now learn to live life that is God-centered!

Out in the world we waste our energy,
now He is in my soul and I hope people see.
Fishing for souls is like fishing in a pond,
with You my Savior I can go beyond!

In your heart, keep Jesus as your stash,
with Jesus NOT there, I surely will crash.
My life was bad & wrong & that is a true story,
time to live for God now & all his Glory!

In life now there is no compromise,
you must go to battle, no matter the size.
Living in this evil world is like a disease,
Living with Jesus now, life goes at ease.

Rusty

Travel To Gloryland

1. Who is in your heart today? (God, woman, friend, child)

2. Has the devil rattled your mind lately?

3. Where is most of your energy spent?

4. Are you going half measures or fully in with Christ?

Notes:

_____
_____
_____
_____
_____
_____
_____

79
Heavenly Home

At times you feel your soul has been molested,
you can't get away, like you were arrested.
Getting you to HELL, is the enemy's goal,
that will all change with Jesus in your soul.

Enemy says "you can't get there cause you are lacking",
but Jesus says "with me, you're never slacking"!
With Jesus inside you go to any length,
you read His word & have His strength.

Oh! that devil he never quits patrolling,
but my sweet Jesus is always controlling.
You lived your life like a slow suicide,
give it ALL to Jesus, you finally decide.

Use to white knuckle it & my teeth were grinding,
now I have Jesus & His love I am finding.
Devil did attack like the nature of the beast,
with Jesus as my best friend, it all has ceased.

My insides now just feel all healthy,
with my Godly tools I am so wealthy.
Police use to hold me for observation,
now with Jesus, I made a heavenly reservation.

Rusty

Heavenly Home

1. What are you lacking today?

2. Are you reading the word and taking the action?

3. Are you going with human or Godly love?

4. Are you healthy INSIDE today?

Notes:

_____

_____

_____

_____

_____

_____

_____

80
Thank You

I really pray your life will get a whole lot brighter,
going God's way helps your heart get lighter!
Now, I must admit Jesus is my boss,
He touched me daily where I wouldn't stay lost.

In my heart, He does attend,
live a good life & don't have to pretend.
Now that you've changed, people throw the past at
them,
today I serve my Jesus with enthusiasm.

I used to live in dissolution,
today I seek out resolution.
At times I walk with Jesus in solitude,
then I learned to live daily with a Godly attitude.

At times He will tell me to be at peace & be quiet,
when it looks like people are fixing to riot.
Now in my soul, my Jesus does dance,
& I love when He puts me in a Godly trance.

He answers my prayers in different ways,
now in my soul is where He stays.
"Thank you Lord" for what you have done,
I can live my life & yes have fun!

Rusty

Thank You

1. Has your heart got lighter?

2. Who is your real BOSS in life?

3. Holy Spirit is in your soul. What do you do to keep him there?

4. Do you have Godly fun in your life?

   Notes:

   _____
   _____
   _____
   _____
   _____
   _____
   _____
   _____

Made in the USA
Las Vegas, NV
13 December 2023

82659991R00102